L I A M

Working A

Published 2020,
Broken Sleep Books:
Cornwall / Wales

brokensleepbooks.com

First Edition

Lay out your unrest.

Publisher/Editor: Aaron Kent
Editor: Charlie Baylis

Typeset in UK by Aaron Kent

Broken Sleep Books is committed to
a sustainable future for our planet,
and therefore uses print on
demand publication.

brokensleepbooks@gmail.com

ISBN: 978-1-913642-09-9

Contents

That's All   7

I'm Beat   8

Pressure of the Udder   9

Assembly   10

Presocial   11

Inside Out   12

Dream Prologue   13

Interlude i   14

The Animal That Therefore I Am   15

Gazing   16

An Interruption to Your Usual Programming   17

With the Ingenuity of Bernard Matthew   18

Apartment Block   19

Metamorphosis   20

Screaming Often Won't Signify Wanting to Go Faster   21

Dream   22

Interlude ii   23

Bestiary   24

MAD   25

Canis Irregularis   26

The Age of Aquarium   27

Snakes Mistake Their Tails for a Snack   28

The Questionable Necessity of Helipads   29

Dream Epilogue   30

Acknowledgements   31

'It is as if I were ashamed… naked in front of this cat, but also ashamed for being ashamed.'

- Jacques Derrida
(translated by David Wills)

Working Animals

Liam Bates

That's All

At the end of every month, assuming
no HR drama, I pull away

the perforated edges of my pay slip. This
signifies my value. It's money to pay

a man to rent a space to sleep, where
I can cool off and heat up ready meals and frozen pizza.

It's a place to order takeaway to. It's a living
room to hold a second hand

leather sofa – someplace to sit and eat
chow mein from a clear plastic tray. Today,

the landlord sent someone round
to set out plastic traps to trick any hungry, hapless rats

– this tactical placing of lipstick-red
boxes, baited toxic. I spent a while thinking

about rat poison's notes of flavour.
Does it fizz like diet pop against the gullet

as it's sinking? This TV politician
is chewing through a kangaroo testicle

for my entertainment. My chow mein
is greasy and bland.

I'm Beat

An hour partitioned into minutes
is three lots of twenty

and twenty's two lots of ten and
a week is a printer chewing paper

till someone from IT comes out to fix it.
Everyone here is much older than me

or maybe we're all the same age now.

Pressure of the Udder

My milk (the blue-topped bottle in the fridge)
is unfit for drinking, so the coffee in my flask

has to be black. I burn my tongue and wince
at the bus windows, fogged thick and dripping

with breath. Someone splutters into their palm
and I picture their death as violent and at my hands.

What kind of divinity am I? Brutish
and spiteful. Damning the unrighteous internally.

The effort of it tires me. I am
purified with a squirt of antibac gel.

Assembly

I helped my parents empty a chunk of their loft,
found a desiccated wasps' nest and a crunchy mound

of dead wasps, picture books and toys hidden
underneath a thick pelt of dust. I stacked

the car full till there was no room for me.
Dad went to the tip by himself with a mass

of swollen bin bags, their forest-green skins taut
and bursting. My childhood didn't even splash

as it landed in the landfill. Gulls assembled overhead.

Presocial

I delivered a spider clenched wet
into the dim of the plughole, stood

above and made sure it was fully washed
away. I sometimes scrub myself raw,

so the tender bathroom air against my body
feels like company. Sometimes

I neglect to shower at all.

Inside Out

Flat pack habitats become
surprisingly sturdy when assembled

exactly according to the diagrams.
Just goes to show, home

is wherever we've bent the earth
up around us. If we could manage

to secure the perimeter...
something keeps arriving at night.

We can hear it sniffing around
the boundaries. Everything

turns monstrous in the dark. We've learned
to still the trembling, to lie there

silent till it leaves.

Dream Prologue

I sleep beneath cotton spreadsheets. A gnat
makes calories of my blood

till I slap it idly dead. Then a nightmare:
(I am) naked and carnal, an object

at the focal centre of a lens.
(I am) grazing on muddy knees, wet

with shame and praying to the grassy
and vegetable ground.

(I am) here to be preyed upon.

Interlude i

Options aplenty available to suit all tastes
and budgets. Pick from marble, oak, pine

or mahogany, with a lining of lace,
flannel, leather, silk, PVC or calico.

Pick acrylic resin or concrete,
epoxy or reinforced steel. Pick glass,

asphalt or Kevlar. Decorated
with a band logo, the livery

of your favourite sports team
or a banner ad for a local business.

Just pick something thick and strong
enough to keep the dirt out.

The Animal That Therefore I Am

Wiping away condensation
to critique your reflection

in a smeared mirror and the cat
slips through the crack in the not-quite-shut door,

catches you standing with your hands full
measuring flesh. An adult cat in the wild

will never *miaow*, but this is not the wild,
this is the bathroom, so suddenly you're aware

of its presence, you're blanching, trying
to cover yourself, but the cat

has always and never been familiar with nudity.

Gazing

Nose pressed flat against the painted wood,
with abs and jaw clenched – the trick to keeping
a creakless weight on the floorboards. You watch
through the fish-eye peephole as your down-the-hall

neighbours arrive home with their child and their arms
full of groceries. You're unsure of the names
of this particular set. You can only recall Tom
at number twelve, who sometimes signs for parcels

when you're not home or you are home
but ignoring the doorbell.

An Interruption to Your Usual Programming

A fat bluebottle vibrato ricochets
round the room's edge till you disturb the circuit

with a rolled tight issue of National Geographic,
with the magazine then unrolled

and repurposed as a shovel to scoop up
the stunned fly to dump it in the pedal bin.

A house spider has built its web where magnolia
wall meets magnolia ceiling. A miniseries

passes by. A spider can be patient.

With the Ingenuity of Bernard Matthew

The rectangle: an efficient shape
for making use of space. Consider
the terrace house. Consider the stacked apartments.
Consider the office block, the cramped

battery hen, stooped under the weight
of its meaty engineering. You stay cooped up,
like an insular Linnaeus, penning
a whispered taxonomy of one.

You name yourself *I*.
Your branch is the whole tree.

Apartment Block

A kestrel hovers above the roadside,
a wary shadow against the sky.

You are stuck handbraked staring
into the arse-end of backlogged traffic.

The sun is a yellow stress ball
out of reach. Up ahead,

a motorcyclist has come apart:
not in the way we all do, but in two

discrete parts – there's the part that's their head
and the part that's not.

You need to piss and you bark
at a drive time radio DJ who isn't listening.

Metamorphosis

Scuttling towards the corner shop for essentials –
baccy, silver rizlas and beer. Hope

the man behind the counter won't strike
a conversation. Led again by a shrinking

four wall necessity to plunge into the affront
that is The Outside. Rain has brought

snails onto the pavement. Their shells
crunch and weep a soft stain on your trainers.

Screaming Often Won't Signify Wanting to Go Faster

The biannual fun fair is in town, feeding
the park with bright noise. It's important

to have fun, you're told, important to cut
loose and hit that healthy work/life balance,

you're told. It's important to relax.
Just relax. Just relax. A strung up

plush husky above the hook-a-duck
represents an unobtainable ideal.

A carousel horse is carried clockwise,
flecked of its colour. You make yourself

queasy on hot dogs and sugar.

Dream

You sleep inside a duvet pupa, warm
and dormant. A dream:

(You are) well fed.
(You are) watered.
(You are) one among many.

Interlude ii

The maggot never calls a meal of dead flesh dinner.
Its mouthparts won't fit round those syllables.
Its poetry is different.

Bestiary

Legless and ratty,
two-legged, pig-headed or ruminant,

four-legged orphans suckle air,
six-legged, singing unripe swan songs,

eight-legged, frightened,
flightless or flighted,

egg and everything,
every one crows around a wormhole.

MAD

The obituaries are blue and bloated. We've given up
on numbering our dead. So very heavy

in our history, holistic in our mourning,
we are sick and gone fission   atom fragments

in a nuclear reactor   fragments

in a warhead.

Canis Irregularis

Sore neck testing the length of Wifi,
we grind and blunt the pointed crowns of our canines

against bone, so pale, wide-eye frenzied
in our feeding. Dogs will eat dogs

if they've forgotten what food looks like.
It's a middle-management-eat-man world

out here, we've forgotten what food looks like,
we've forgotten which berries are sweet good,

which berries are bitter bad, we've suspended
the seasons in freeze-frame salt.

The Age of Aquarium

More and more born into hereditary psychosis
with instincts at odds with circumstance,

spun dizzy and wretched – we are seasick
but the exact opposite, quaking on tremolo limbs.

We are retching on schedules, performing
daily for an audience of faceless and insatiable gods.

We thrash in our tanks, so much tighter
in circumference than the ocean.

Snakes Mistake Their Tails for a Snack

We see the act for what it is. A shovelling
of dirt from one spot to another

and then back again. Forgot the purpose
but at some point stopped questioning,

certain we once found ourselves a sustenance
in the soil,

become ash, become brattish and spoiled
as in decaying.

The Questionable Necessity of Helipads

Like milk from earlier, the calendar sours.
The clock is a trough full of swill.

If we decline to swim or eat,
we could spill past the rim, we could kill time

all at once. Done with increments,
we could reshape the hour in our image.

See the sun's here sometimes and it's light
and at other times it's not, it's dark. That's all.

Dream Epilogue

Kept awake by the drone, the laboured breathing,
of the landscape, we map a crowfly path,

follow best we can to soothe the din,
to mute the wheezing and wander till we blister feet

and ease the droning sleepless, ceaseless ache.

Out here,

where a moment's less contaminated,
we can reach up tiptoe, fingers stretched

to stroke a constellation, or reach out
straight in front to touch something cognate

something reaching, like we are.

Acknowledgements

I always intended these poems to be read as a whole, so
they've not appeared anywhere else individually. I do
though have to thank everyone who took a look at earlier
versions – Roger Robinson, Isabelle and Freya at Fly on the
Wall Press, and of course Katie, who planted the seed for this
idea in the first place.

I've got to also acknowledge Jacques Derrida, whose book
'The Animal That Therefore I Am', gave me an epigraph, an
idea, and a poem title. And finally I'd like to thank Alias and
Doseone, whose album 'Less Is Orchestra' I listened to A
LOT during the making of this.

LAY OUT YOUR UNREST